2 Kinds
Of Fire

2 KINDS OF FIRE

PORSCHE KELLY

www.thepoeticactivist.com

ISBN: 978-0-578-56187-5

Illustrations and Cover Design by
Wella Lee

For Granny

I did it.

TABLE OF CONTENTS

PREFACE

I've learned that freedom can only be obtained if there is first honesty. Often times we try to live life, leaving the past in the past and convincing ourselves that we are walking in freedom. But without facing our past in truth and transparency, how can we truly live? In my opinion, it is impossible to leave behind that which still dangles right in front of you.

It took me a while to let this book fly into the hands of the world. There were times I took pieces of it out simply because I was not ready to reveal things about myself. I battled with whether I was revealing too much or not going deep enough. But after meditating and sitting in complete silence, talking with God, and hearing wisdom from those I respect most, I heard this: If only one person is touched by the words you bravely weave together, you've done your job.

Years ago, my late granny and I made a pact. I told her that her story needed to be told and that she needed to write a book. She sat quiet for a minute or two then said "Ok, if you write your book, I'll write mine." Though she is no longer here with me, I figured my gift to this world, and to her, would be to finally write the book.

This is my life, story, and testimony. It is a diary I felt God urging me to share; a place where I've kept my secret agony and disappointments and let the sun shine on them so that someone else could see that not only do others fall, make mistakes, and hurt too, but they also grow and triumph. This is what the enemy is afraid of: people staring in the face of shame and yelling their truth with no apology. Telling the world about all my ugly is a weapon that will destroy chains people are bound by. Let my story help free you. Then let it inspire you to tell yours and help free someone else.

I'm a firm believer in silver linings. Storms and hard rain mean eventually a rainbow is coming. I finally got to see my rainbow. I pray one day you see yours too.

ACKNOWLEDGMENTS

To Thomas & Adrienne Kelly, Bettigene Johnson, Adele Stewart, Reggie & Demetra Mack, Roy & Marion Overall, Charles & Erika Price, Steven & Portia Sumner, Katy Wade, Dawn Humphrey, Jeralyn Dayon, Lomika Sojourner, Patrick & Courtney Miller, Semaj Miller: you have been instrumental and vital to my growth, standing with me through the pretty and the ugly and each of you has spoken life into me when I needed it most. Thank you.

I've played with the wrong kind of fire.
Got burned so bad, I thought I would never recover.

But I've also walked through fires I owe my life to.
Fires that didn't consume me.
Couldn't consume me.

After all,
I wasn't in it alone.

PSALM

ONE THIRTY NINE

THIRTEEN

LISTEN

I debated whether or not to tell you
About the break ups
About the abuse
About the depression
About the sin
About the ugly
I debated whether or not to risk shame
To risk judgment
To risk eyes looking at me
Differently
But screw it
I'll tell you everything

BIRTHED

Timer set
9 months baking
Recipe called for 1 part statistic
2 parts love
Swam around in Black Sea
Somersaults and backflips
Ready to see the world
I was her world

Painted marks on skin and made it stretch
Wider than normal
Made pretty feet swell
Made good food smell
Made morning sickness a part
of her daily routine

But push time comes, no performance enhancers
Au naturel
Pain proved itself worthy
I was worthy

Brown eyes stare wide eyed into tear drops
She did it, I did it, we did it
Banner hangs across her face
Welcome home

Her eyes whisper words of wisdom
As smiles stream down

World can get chaotic
World can get too much to handle
Don't worry
Make it, you will
Strong willed, like mama
Stop you, nothing can
Brown eyes stare wide eyed

TO DO LIST

Wake up
Put pants on backwards
Place shoe on the wrong foot
Cry
Replace tears with smiles
Jacket becomes ticket out of door
Hold mama's hand
Find the book at the library
The yellow one with the chickens
Cheese for mama's memories
Cheat on the book of chickens
For the sand in the box
Cook mud pies
Get yelled at for trying to eat
Work out calves on swing
Sing purple dinosaur songs
Ask to stay longer
Ask again and again
Walk back home
Force dad to read about chickens
Soon as he walks through the door
Ask for something other than brussel sprouts
Pout while eating brussel sprouts
Cry
Replace tears with smiles
Finishing dinner is ticket to fun
Before night light time
Find Snuggles the bear
Sneak into mom's purse
Draw red marker on face
Jump when mom finds you
On floor with red marker
That isn't really marker

Cry
Replace tears with smiles
Arms carry you to bed
Night light time
Stare at glow in the dark stars on ceiling
Fight sleep
Fight sleep
Fight sleep
Close eyes, new day, repeat

SINISTER

In kindergarten
I bothered the big kids
My cousin ran out of the classroom
To save me from the ones
Who took my arms and legs and spun me around
Out of anger
This is what mama feared
Brain smart enough to start school early
Brain not mature enough to leave kids alone
I guess they didn't like being bullied by a toddler

In 1st grade
Papa picked me up from school
I said goodbye to my friend
Gave her the friendliest tug on her braids
Made her cry
I guess she didn't like her hair being pulled

In 3rd grade
The bell rang
Rose lost her tooth in class
I took Rose's tooth after class
Laughed
Ran down the staircase as she chased me outside
Tossed it in the bush
She never found it
She screamed
No visit from the Tooth Fairy
I guess she didn't like her things being taken

In 4th grade
They played foursquare
The ball rolled in front of me

They reached out their arms with smiles
Wanted me to throw it back
I took it
Kicked it so far, you could call it a home run
They went and told on me
I guess they didn't like my idea of a joke

In middle school
In high school
In college
I mean mugged the world
Told human beings to beware with my eyes
Tried to show them being 5'1 is not grounds
To make me feel small

In adulthood I found out
I stood up to folks
Bit hands that just wanted to say hi
Bullied
Rejected
Before they could first reject me

HAIR

They would ask me
How come I never wore my hair down
Let the wind whisper in it
They didn't know
How many hot combs
Relaxers
Sit stills
Head turns
Hours
Cringing
I had to endure
I told them
But they didn't believe me
They just laughed at the afro puff I wore everyday

ONE OF THE BOYS

Growing up
I liked to be one of the boys
Four square
Kickball
Track
I didn't feel like gossiping
About who liked who
I'd rather come home
With bruises
Skinned knees from letting my body
Become one with the ground
I did play with Barbies
But I'd make them fight
Put them in a ring of my imagination
And make them solve their problems
With open hands
I don't remember when it happened
The moment I hurt myself
Became woman
And allowed my sleeves to be covered
In blood from my heart

REALITY

Had they told me
I'd go from running from my shadow
Playing in the dirt
Picking up toys
To cutting up my hands
Picking up pieces of my shattered heart
off the floor
I would've stayed young

OREO

I spoke proper English
Danced with ebonics ever so often
But I often let the enunciation of my r's and g's cut in
I stayed in my books
Sometimes passed on playing outside to sit inside to make Powerpoint presentations and take typing tests on Mavis Beacon
Just for fun
A lover of Microsoft Office in elementary school
I rushed in front of the TV every night to get lost in Jeopardy
Watched Pride & Prejudice
The old one on VHS
Made myself into a walking dictionary
The one folk used to consult about all things spelling
I grew up on MJ, and Clark Sisters, and
Kirk Franklin and Brandy and Mac Dre and all things Oakland
But I faithfully knew the words to Linkin Park and Aerosmith and Phil Collins and Michelle Branch

Watched every episode of Friends at least 10 times
Not to mention classical music was life
Made me pick up the piano and violin
I slapped Bach and Beethoven
Obsessed over Moonlight Sonata and Canon in D and The Chairman's Waltz
I spent too much time reading Harry Potter and R.A. Salvatore
I didn't get a chance to memorize the lines to Friday or Dead Presidents
Nor did I own a single pair of Jordans

So they called me oreo
A black girl
Whose taste in everything
Made her white

DON'T LIE

Life ain't all sunshine and rainbows
I would willingly do the time
if I stood here and lied

Mask on
Smiling with lips that have tasted pain
thick enough to suffocate the strongest of souls

I know what it is to water a garden
Wake up the next morning expecting
blooms and be surprised with a sea
of thorns

I know what it is to anticipate the golden
of July and be given the frost bite
of December

I know what it is to drown in 1 foot
of water
To fall out of a window 36 inches
from the ground
To be hit in the head with a feather
and slip into a coma

Life ain't all sunshine and rainbows
I would tape the lids over my eyes shut
Before I stare into yours and lie
Don't lie
Don't lie
You been through some things too

GRASS AIN'T GREENER

I finally built a ladder out of my envy and
complaining
Every day a piece of metal flung to its foundation
from my mind and lips quick to ship out negativity
from the dock

Attempts to swim to shore blown away by the
drowning in oceans of greener grass in the
neighbors' yard
I finally opened my eyes

Looked around, and saw my ocean filled
with bodies
Lullabies carried in the wind
Sing tunes of she has more
He has more
They have more
I want more

Nobody is happy
Looked around and saw my ocean filled with bodies
They drown too

STRENGTH

They hear the power in my voice
Admire it
Adore it
Wish for it
They don't know
How many times
I had to go hoarse to get it

IMMUNITY

Open up the book that is me
Read all my pages
Before you start playing with assumption's fire

Just because I grew up in a 2 parent household
Ate breakfast, lunch, & dinner daily
Don't mean I've never been broken

PROTECTION

They said no
I couldn't spend the night
Like everybody else
They saw things happen
They didn't want them to happen
To me
Fast forward 10 years
They happened anyway

CYCLOPS

I remember a time when I was about 12
Sitting in my room on the floor
Eyes glaring at my skin as if I were Cyclops
Wishing for the ability to burn off
My flesh
Praying
God
Please make me anything
But black

BLACK GIRL

Black girl scared of her own reflection.
Society's definition of beauty don't align with
black girl's image so, black girl's perception of
her black face is imperfection.
In her mind, black girl mean imperfection.
Black girl mean undesired complexion.
Black girl mean turn around wrong direction.
Black girl mean mistake need correction.
Black girl mean last, no one's first selection.
Black girl mean rejection.
Black girl get treated like infection.
Black girl scared of her own reflection.
So black girl tiptoes past broken mirrors, shields
her face near windows, avoids eye contact with
her own shadow.

As brown eyes pierce television screens wondering
why Disney never make princesses with original
stories whose skin color match black girl.
Black girl on verge of breaking down during recess
as friends question why her black hair always
chained, always restrained into puff ball.
Black girls friends don't understand what Just For
Me perms are.
Never owned toothless combs or knockerballs or
Pro Style Gel.

Black girl see others' hair as free, black hair as jailed.
Imprisoned, limited.
Black girl sick of it.
Black girl pool of shame, black girl dips in it.
Black girl glimpse of hope, the world sticks a pin in
it.

Dark skinned black girl traded for a lighter Vivian.
Black girl envies other black girls 50 shades lighter,
50 shades brighter.

Black girl clench her 50 shades dark fists
tighter.
Black girl wish she was 50 shades whiter.
Black girl ashamed of her black frame.
Ashamed of her black name.
Ashamed of her black ways.
Black girl mind work like pendulum, swing
back and forth, back and forth between sadness and
joy.
Black girl not even wanted by black boy.
Movie, tv, video, black girl equals black toy.

Black girl too black, black girl not black enough.
Black girl too strong, black girl not tough enough.
Black girl unsupported, existence distorted, pretty
brown neck, with chains the world adorns it.
Black girl exiled from her land & replaced with
phonies.
Black girl mean Nina Simone gets played by Zoe.

Black girl, sin.
Black girls can't win.
But black girls' lips and booties are always in.
Black girl mean catch 22.
Black girl mean lose-lose.
Who stand up for the black girl?

Crickets.
No sound, deafening silence.
Black girl victim of emotional violence.
She too loud, too hard, too thick, too this
too that.
I mean, black girls are just too black.

The blacker the berry, the sweeter the pain,
black girl stay in your own lane.

But, what does it profit a black girl to gain
acceptance in this world and lose her black soul?
Black girl, your black hair, skin, & soul is beautiful.
Black girl now know she is beautiful.
Beautiful flower, long pretty stem.
Black girl no hard rock, black girl gem, brown skin,
extra melanin, French kissed by the sun, it glistens
off your skin.
Black girl glows.
Black girl's confidence grows.
Black girl's confidence shows.
Black girl fine.
Straight hair.
Dreads.
Bald.
Fro.
Braids.
Twists.
Black girl please know:
We don't need remi or yaki to have it going on.

In strength & dignity black girl is clothed.
Black girl like phoenix, black girl rose from the
ashes this world attempted to burn her into.
Spread your extra pigmented wings and fly.
Black girl rise.
Black girls unite.
Black girls get into formation, black girls fight.
Black girl be emancipated from mental slavery.
Black girl drop that fear and pick up bravery.

Black girl no make believe.
Black girl magic & black girl real.
Black girl you know the deal.

We don't need the mass appeal.
See, this is black girl power.
Black girl this your hour, your time.
Let your light, caramel, dark, or bluest black skin
shine, shine black girl.

From the Assata Shakurs to the Angela Davises,
all shades beautiful complexion.
Black girl needs no correction.
Black girl, black skin, perfection.
Black girl smiles back at her own reflection.

WALLS

They used to think I was mean
The girl who be mean muggin' everybody
They didn't understand
Opening up
Was like walking on a tightrope
Over an ocean of dolphins
And sharks
Sometimes it's hard to tell
Who is safe

PSALM
SIX
SIX

DEPRESSION

She thought she had to suck it up
Fix her face
Make her shoulders smile
Get it together
Suppress her feelings
The show must go on

JAZMINE

I didn't but I wish I did
Channeled my inner Jazmine
Let every stroke of the brick that sat outside
Sing melodies all over his mode of transportation
I wanted my hands to slow dance on the inside
Tear everything apart like he did me
How he rid me of everything but these ugly scars
I wish I could have called her
Asked her how she did it
Left her initials with the crowbar
But I heard she was the one still crying
All I could do was sign mine on his heart
Cross it and hope he'd...

EVERY 98 SECONDS

You ever be in such shock
You try to make yourself vomit "no"
Force it out of your half eaten soul
Wish someone would blow their rape whistle
And rescue you
But in the moment
You still can't believe what's happening
And your lips are stitched shut?
Me neither

JUST MOLESTED

Somebody told me
Go to one of those groups
The ones you pull up to in secret
Where victims spill a little of themselves
On the floor
Cry together and eat cake after
I told them I didn't get raped
Only thing penetrated was my soul
I was just molested
I didn't know just was such a powerful word

IT'S OK

Happy New Year.
I should have stopped kissing him.
That clear liquid that made my limbs go numb.
I think his name was Tequila.

Had I been more me I would have seen it coming.
Had I not been weak I'd have seen you coming.
That friendly face I'd known to never swat a fly.

Turned terror. Turned terrorist. Turned extra terrestrial.
An alien like being with tentacles long enough to keep
my vocal chords on mute.

Eyes so heavy with a desperation to burst into tears.
But the fear was so real I could only cry on the inside.

Lungs, feeling as though they'd been filled with water.
Just let me drown in my own sorrow.

I can't watch this anymore.
I no longer knew what it was.
I no longer knew who he was.
I no longer knew where I was.

How much longer will paralysis dance over my body,
spinning pirouettes as every text my brain tries to send
to my sleeping muscles is intercepted.

Wake up, something's not right.
How much longer can my no, no, no's be snatched
from the air and turned into a pool of nothingness.

How much longer can I yell at the top of my broken

lungs with no alarm sounding to wake the others.
Were there others.
Bodies you tore asunder.
Bodies you held under water, drown fast gasp for
breath.
How much longer, I wonder.

How would I face your mother on Sunday at church
when she tries to hug me. Smiles and tells me I look
lovely but I just want to scream, your son, he touched
me and now every part of me from the inside to the
out   feels ugly. And when I lay down at night my
dreams are seizures foaming with haunting thoughts
and I wake up feeling yucky.

I've never worn clothes and felt so naked.
You wore clothes but still felt naked.
I never knew you were so heavy. I wasn't ready. For
your body to pin me to the floor.

I'm breathless. I'm restless.
Seemed like hours had passed until you were finished.
Sexual violation, mark that off my checklist.

The liquor made me reckless. It's me not you. This is
on me not you. Like last night when you were on me.

I can't think.
I can't see.
I'm blinded by the memory of a white popcorn ceiling.
Staring. Judging. Laughing. Asking.

Why I was so irresponsible.
Why I didn't see it coming.
Why I didn't see you coming.
A bee buzzing at the smell of my nectar. Asking.
If I really didn't want it, how come I made no attempt

at running.

Sunrise.
Let's eat breakfast.
Let's act pleasant.
Let's be selfish.
Let's play fantasy.
Make believe nothing happened.
Because nothing really happened.
And you didn't mean it.
And I accept it.
And my common sense was neglected.
And had I been sober, I'd have been protected.
And who really ever gets justice for just being molested.
And I'm embarrassed.

Preparing myself to lose it all in this storm of never ending thunder.
My mind.
My sanity.
My boyfriend to women who won't cringe when he attempts to hug her.

Let's play hide and seek.
You hide from the truth.
I'll seek for answers.

Why me. Why me. Why you. Why now.
It's ok.
I'll be ok.
We'll be ok.

SHAME

When I called my dad to tell him what happened

To tell him that someone had stolen my body

I beat around the bush

Separated my lips one staple at a time

As if I would get in trouble

As if I did something wrong

SEXUAL ASSAULT

It's almost like
Watching prey be half eaten
By its predator
Then turning on itself
To finish the job

THERAPY

It's foreign in the land of black women
That "and how do you feel about that" BS
That's for the white folk
We learned to Erykah Badu our mess
Carry it with us
Rather be bag lady
Than sit in front of some random
Tellin em'
How much it hurts to smile

BEST FRIEND

We had a long standing appointment
Daily meetings in dusty darkness
Morning
Afternoon
Night
Repeat
Feasted on emptiness and salty tears
Exchange of words
Rare
Mind
Bare of thoughts worth thinking
I felt like sinking
He cradled me
Until next time
The corner was my best friend

2ND

The reason I always strived
for 1st

Was because somebody always made me 2nd

READY OR NOT

He told me he wasn't ready
He forgot to tell me
He was ready for someone else

RECIPE FOR INSANITY

I'd rip out my heart, along with all of my trust
Carefully place it in the most expensive box
Wrap it with ribbon and tears and anger
Hand deliver

I always went out of my way to give my everything
I'd ring the door bell and wait for his heart to answer
But it never did

He'd just glance out of a broken window
until I turned away, dark clouds on my face
As I swore to God and my womanhood
I would never do this again

And then my lonely would kick in
And his deaf ears suddenly could hear
But only when the sound of my feet
walking away grew louder than his ego

He'd give me a piece of him
A piece of him that was barely enough
to keep me warm, whisper sorry
And I'd rip out my heart again,
along with all of my trust
Ready to hand deliver
Ready to go out of my way
to give my everything
Just to receive another glance
out of a broken window
and 100 more sorries

TODAY

Today
I watched an old video
My brain said it was me
Laughing
Dancing
Joking
The life of the party
Too much death in me now
My heart couldn't recognize her

OIL IS TO WATER

I know He want me to be real
God
But I told Him no
I can't let them know
That sometimes my body
Wants to take permanent naps
That good sleep you don't want to wake up from,
literally

My mind says
Christian is to depression
As oil is to water
They don't mix

WAR

Waking up felt like getting a paper cut

Rolling out of bed felt like burning a tongue

Walking out the door felt like going off to war

SOMETIMES, CHRISTIANS
GET DEPRESSED TOO

Last Sunday I stood in the front
Reached to heaven with stilt arms
I made my feet dance
Cried out in 3 million tongues
And held hands with the Holy Spirit Himself

I sat down in the 1st row
Turned to my neighbor every time Pastor said so
I was so tuned in and focused on church

Pretended not to notice Lucifer's spirit lurk
in my direction
Had to whisper Isaiah 41:10 a couple times
for protection

I used my phone to take notes
I took good notes too, on Pastor's word
Word was so good , I couldn't sit still
I stood up, clapped, yelled mmhmm and come on
until my voice grew tired
I felt my spirit rewire into the system its maker
intended

Service ends
I even went and hugged the one who
offended me
I laughed with my friends
Made Sunday lunch plans

And then I drove home, speeding
To return to my cage of broken
Sat alone and had Psalms 42:3 for dinner

A bowl of salty tears from eyes
that angrily cried
Wondered why
Wondered if they was blind
Cuz they couldn't see the God
My brain told them to see
Couldn't understand the concept
of the evidence of things unseen

I got up from the couch and had dessert
in my room
A spoonful of the sweetest agony
I put on my Jeremiah robe
and rocked myself to Lamentations
I stayed up long past my bed cry
Bed time
Dread time
The time I'd dread going to sleep
Where my dreams would come for me
When I ain't send for them
I pretend for them

When they ask me how I'm doing
Look in my purse and pull out my
"blessed and highly favored"
My "won't He do it"
My "I don't know why they don't serve Him"

Are they still watching
Soon as they stop watching
The people I stay trying to please
I put all my masks back into my bag
Knowing good and well I don't feel favored
Knowing good and well I feel like I'm in labor
Birthing a fetus with close resemblance to
Loneliness
Indifference

Rejection
Blank

You ever had an invisible gun pointed
at your temple
Hoped it wasn't filled with blanks
You ever draw a blank
Not able to remember all the good things
He's already done for you
Me too
Deep down I love Jesus
This I know
He love me too
But all lying aside
Sometimes Christians get depressed too

JEALOUS

Sometimes I'm jealous of them

The others

The ones that aren't here anymore

The ones

on the other side

CAESAR: A POEM ABOUT SUICIDE

People tell me my dog is out of control. A cute ball of fur whose spirit does not match his outward appearance. The epitome of don't judge a book by its cover. If you approach him too fast, he may lunge. They say I let him run the house. I say, I know.

I remember on his 1st birthday, someone asked me to hang out. I said no, I had a party to plan. They asked "whose?" I said "Caesar's." They laughed.

I remember all the comments I got from the picture of his cake that I made from scratch frosted with peanut butter and love, garnished with a C made out of carrots and my soul. "Did you really light a candle for a dog?" they said. "Do you really let him sleep in your bed?" they said. "That's that white people stuff."

They didn't know that this little mixed breed constantly barking at everything walking, refusing to put on his collar when it's time to go, growling like a savage when I tell him give me the chicken bone he got out of the garbage saved me from myself.

They don't know. I used to sit on the couch, staring at cream walls I thought were smiling evilly, sitting in empty corners full of eyes, rolled into a ball, lying on a bed of thorns, singing to my thoughts tunes of "would it be so bad if I were no longer here?"

They don't know I would go to work and whisper to my feet "today is the day you will finally, accidentally, walk in front of the bus." They don't know that sometimes when I was with them, I wasn't really with them.

It was my black body playing dress up. Dressing up as normal. Dressing up as life is a box of chocolates. Dressing up as strong. Because being black means you don't have emotional heart attacks. Brown skin means depression does not exist. See, we don't go to therapists, just suck it up and get over it.

They don't know. He would come in my house and crouch, arms out, smelling like the brimstone from which he'd come, saying "just come to papa" and I'd contemplate his offer as I stared at a drawer of sharp blades, humming to myself sweet dreams must be made of this.

They don't know that I so believe that the God I believe in further proved himself when He sent me that lady, who no longer wanted the cute ball of fur, whose spirit did not match his outward appearance. They don't know that I too was a ball of false strength whose spirit did not match her outward appearance.

When an animal has a way of making you feel like life is worth living more than any human can, you realize how stupid you can look for baking him a cupcake with frosting and love and carrots and soul and a candle and care not what they may think. You realize your words become a shield battling their swords dipped in "it's just a dog" flames.

So, a cupcake and my covers covered in Chihuahua Terrier follicles is the least I can offer him for helping me stay.

STILL HERE

I still got healing to do
Still got some things to go through
Some lessons to learn
Some pain
To cry through
Scream through
Fight through
Walk through
Some doors to close
And never open again
Some folk to make invisible
Some lies to erase with truth
I still got healing to do
But at least I'm still here

PSALM
FORTY ONE
NINE

THIS THING

I do this thing
Where I look to people for oxygen
Barely breathing

Walk through life ill
Clasping onto creation instead of the creator

I do this thing
Where I put people in God's place

Then wonder why
I'm still sick

FRIENDS WITH A NIGHTMARE

When I was younger, about 7 years old
I had a friend that wouldn't go away
I heard he was friends with a lot of people
Some called him sleep paralysis
I called him something else
He only wanted to talk to me at night

I would close my eyes and there he was
A magician
Making appear a never ending ocean of covers
I could not claw my way out of
I felt like Ariel
The way he Ursula-ed my voice

I remember trying to scream
Jesus
But it was almost as if my mouth didn't know Him
Sometimes I would try to stay awake all night
so that my body could smile but my heavy eyelids
helped him come back

Then I grew up
And my friend only came to visit me a couple times
as an adult
And now after 27 years of life on Earth
I look back at every i.v. of pain that was pushed
into my veins
Everyone who hurt me
And I think about how my friend
The one they call sleep paralysis but I call
something else
Was a better friend to me than some of my old ones
At least with him, I knew what to expect

BACKSLIDE

We'd worship in secret
Threw Exodus 20:4 in the trash
And became God in each other's eyes
Idols
Took our lust
Carefully placed it in the bottom drawer
On the left
Keep it hidden
We got church in the morning

FORNICATION

Sex be feeling good
That premarital kind
Til you wake up
Feeling emptier
Than before your
"We can't"
Turned into
"Ok"

VALUES

If I chose not to do things
Because I valued myself
The way God said He do
Versus fearing right and wrong
Or what mama might say
I'd still be a virgin

SOUL TIES

Society is funny
Talks about things
Like body count
How many partners have you slow danced with

The only number that matters
Is the one soul you allow
To be dangerously tangled with others
Yours

MYSPACE

We told them we met at Lucky
In aisle 7
It was a sunny day

That story set the tone
For the rest of our broken
Lucky always sounded better than Myspace
Lies always sounded better than truth

MOMMY ISSUES

I finally got to see the way
you treat your mother and it all made sense
Why "bitch"
Was such a huge part of your vocabulary
Why your love language was talking
with hands and ugly
How could you ever have respect for any woman
on this earth
If you would bring harm to the very womb
that gave you breath
How could I ever have respect
For you
For myself
If I continued to say
It's ok
I know he didn't mean it

MY FIRST

My first time
Was with a boy
Who once pushed me into a table
Told me to get up and stop being dramatic
It wasn't that much blood
It wasn't that much love
I asked him
Why he was so angry
He told me I could leave
I did
Then I came back the next day

IMPURE

I skipped class
Caught 2 BART trains and 1 bus
Walked a few blocks
Lost
Myself
My mind
My purity
Got an F in Anthropology
I never went to the lab
All to give the gift God gave me
Away to the man
Whose pet name for me
Became female dog

LIAR

I be having my gun ready
Loaded with as many remember when you saids
As possible
For the next one act like he better than the last
The one who say I would never do that to you
The one who ridicule the ones come before him
The one who say he'll protect me
Then turn around and be exactly
Who you asked him not to be

OCEANS

Into oceans
I have dived deep
for people who wouldn't even allow their feet
to meet the surface for me

CONDEMNATION

I once wanted to pray for someone
Felt like God was telling me to
Then he interrupted
The evil one
Said I had no right to pray after what I did last night

YES

If I would have known
The hands you used
To dress my finger with that ring
Would continue to be
The same hands
You use to undress other women
I would have never said yes

ALARMS

He was a house I had no business
moving into, let alone setting foot in
Beautiful on the outside
Broken and worn on the inside

Mama said never date potential
Don't let your eyes be hypnotized by
the flowers in the front yard
Make sure the house don't just
look good, but is stable
Feels like home

He was a house I had no business
moving into, let alone setting foot in
God became arsonist
Set it on fire to get my attention
Smoke alarms went off in every room
to wake me up

I reluctantly picked up my body
Carried it outside in slow motion
and got my sight back
Then ran right back inside to grab some things
I should have let burn

ILL

I woke up feeling sick
Tried to make myself throw up
Drove myself to insanity
As I swam in my memory's ocean
To find the source
I laid back down with you
It never dawned on me
That the medicine I wanted you to be
Was actually the poison
That made me ill

NAIVE

At one point, you could have told me
you loved me then shot me in the heart
seconds after, and I would have died
believing you anyway.

BECAUSE

I thought
He loved me
Was always there
That
He was someone
While the other one ignored me
He was my comfort
That turned into a bed
That turned into a kiss
That turned into a hug
I just needed a shoulder
Repeatedly
After all, it was done to me first
I didn't call it cheating
It's because
When I knew it was wrong
The guy at work
I gave myself to him
If you ask me why

-Backwards poem

WORK CLOTHES

What I wore on the outside to work
Wasn't nearly as important
As what I was wearing underneath
I wasn't going there to do my job anyway
I was going to do something else

SUPERPOWER

When they ask that same old question
To break ice
If you could have any super power
What would it be
Give me the ability to see
Into the future
That way
I'd be able to run fast when I see death coming

TOY STORY

I know what it's like
To be that doll in the corner
Once shiny, new
Now used
Never shown to the world
Only the star of the show
In the shadows
Only come alive when nobody's looking
He only wanna play in secret
When the other one ain't available

WHAT TO DO WHEN YOU
GET ENGAGED

A list of things to do when you get engaged:
Cry tears of joy.
Post a picture on Instagram to let everyone know
you got engaged.
Cry tears of joy.
Forget about the ultimatum you hit him over the
head with and just be happy he finally did it.
Try to go to sleep.
Wake up the next morning to see how many people
liked the picture of you getting engaged.
Spend hours at work saving Pinterest wedding ideas
you probably won't use.

Set a date.
Create a guest list.
Revise the guest list to add people who will probably
get offended if they aren't invited, regardless of the
fact that at any other time they would barely
whisper your name, let alone speak to you.
Revise the guest list again once you realize this
is your day and good food ain't cheap.

Listen to your future mother and sister in law
tell people a rumor.
The one where you set the date on a day they
couldn't make, on purpose.

Go into your fiancé's email and find his matches
for dating sites.
Confront your fiancé about his matches for dating
sites.

Watch his mouth spill stagnant water.
A breeding ground for contamination and lies.

Take out your broom made of pride and
embarrassment, then sweep all issues under
the rug.
Hide the rug when guests come over.

Find a wedding venue.
Ask your parents to help you pay for the venue.
Put down a deposit.
Take engagement photos.
Pretend you're happy in the engagement photos.
Don't let the photographer see the cracks in
your smile.

Empty your pockets of money and dignity to lend
to your fiancé.
Money that probably helped pay for your own ring.
Cry tears of sadness.
Try on wedding dresses.
Cry tears of joy that quickly turn into sadness
when you remember the secrets you found
in a locked phone.
A phone you apparently had no business going
in, according to him.

Roll your eyes when your dad loves on you
in the form of are you sure.
In the form of correction.
Of concern.
Tell your dad you know what you're doing,
knowing you don't know what you're doing.

Pose in front of your marriage counselors.
Lie to them.

Feed them gardens of roses and tulips and marigolds.
Don't show them the weeds growing underneath.
Talk to them in the hallway but don't let them
all the way in.
Make sure you don't give them any ammo of truth
to shoot down your engagement.

Stay up all night wondering where he is.
Knowing he's with her, or her, or maybe with
the other her.
Go to work and cry. Everyday.
Trade your tears in for moments of love that aren't
really love from the guy across the hall.
At least he cares about you more than your fiancé.

Enjoy your bridal shower.
Walk into the room with all of the women in
your life ready to tell them you aren't happy and
you want out. Then tell yourself to suck it up.
Maybe things will change once you say I do.

Have your mentors sit you down.
See the apology on their faces and know without
their lips moving your life is over.
Listen to them read you a bedtime story
you've heard before.
The one about you being cheated on, again.
This time in another country.

Call off the wedding 1 month before.
Put the invitations to your funeral back in the box.
Lose your parents' deposit on the wedding venue.
Feel sorry for your bridesmaids who spent money
on sackcloth disguised as dresses for your happily
never after.
Put your wedding dress in the garage on the same
shelf as your shame.

Miss your friends' engagement party 2 weeks later.
14 days isn't enough time to come out of hiding.
Opt out of your speech at your best friend's
wedding, because how dare you speak about love
when you have none.
When you lost one.
Or at least what you thought was.

Fall into depression.
Isolate yourself.
Scream "I wish I listened".
Sulk.
Scream "I wish I listened".
Sulk.

Fight for your life.
Ask God to help you remember who you were
before you dropped yourself on the ground.
Ask Him to remind you of the image He created
you in that does not look like your ex.
Fight for your life.
Sulk.
Scream "I wish I listened."
Fight for your life.
Sulk.
Scream "I wish I listened."

WHITE DRESS
BLACK SOUL

Here comes the almost bride. Here comes the high tide washing empty dreams away. No need to call the fire department. The building of false hope has already been burnt to ash and no phoenix will be rising from this dust.

I must say, it has been a hell of a ride.
Excuse me, I mean a hell of a lie. 1, 2, 3, 4, 5 years time and I've watched it all die. But what's funny is that the deceased was actually dead a long time ago. The skeletons are just now being let out of the closet. I would have rather cried rivers of anguish beneath weekday specific masks than to let you know I was hurting.

Sunday comes and I put on that masked smile. They ask when I'll be walking down the aisle. I tell them through clenched teeth that I'm waiting for the love I give to be reciprocated. I'm waiting for the other half to be as dedicated to me as Kaepernick is to taking a knee at every game.

We played games. And not the fun kind like Operation or Twister or Uno. Games like Sorry & Trouble & BS & even Monopoly where you have no idea what you're doing yet you continue to play because you feel stuck but finally you've had enough of losing and you swipe all the pieces off the board to even the score, no more.

I used to be haunted by the cries of loneliness. Single was a curse word. Forget about my happiness and joy. Let me put my Barbie face on and pretend my heart is a toy to be played with.

Pride was my coat of many colors. And I didn't need any brothers to toss me in a ditch, I did that on my own.

Too afraid of being alone. Too afraid of leaving my comfort zone. Too afraid of my sisters getting shiny jewelry on the 4th finger of their left hands before me. I had to beat them. How could I let their 1 year relationship turn into real commitment before my never ending story? And if my soul happened to be killed in the crossfire, then so be it. At least I'd get to wear a pretty white dress and keep pretending I'm ok for one special day.

I now take you to be my lawfully unfaithful husband.
In sickness & in health.
Until you become the death of me.
Until you finally get the best of me.
Until nothing is left of me.
Have you ever experienced a loveless love?
How contradictory.
Here comes the almost bride dressed in white.
With a black soul.

IN LAWS

If he can't tell his mother
And his sister
To stop calling you a female dog
And other things
On social media
Get rid of him

MUSIC

I hate when songs remind you of someone you're
taking

space from

Some of my favorite songs I once vibed to
later made

my ears bleed

THE BLACK WOMAN

If I had a dime for every time they lied

Pretended to be hurt while begging for forgiveness they'd later take for granted

Said sorry for the same evil they ironically defined as an honest mistake

I would still be the most disrespected, unprotected person in America

CHURCH

Sitting in church the day after you finish telling God "screw you" with your actions is painful.

Imagine doing it every Sunday.

COLLECTION

He said
"I'm not like him"
I took his lie and added it to my collection
Framed it and put it on the wall
Made it the next trinket on my charm bracelet
Placed it in my hall of fame
At least each player
Sounded more sincere
Than the one before

REAP

The other day,
I remembered that one time I kissed someone in high school.

A someone that belonged to one of my best friends.

By the time I realized I forgot to put my lies back in their hiding place, delete the texts, my phone told her eyes all the secrets.

"You doin' me scandalous", she said with her mouth. Her eyes. Her heart.

10 years later, by the time he realized he forgot to put his lies back in their hiding place, delete the texts, his phone told my eyes all the secrets.

"You doin' me scandalous", I said with my mouth. My eyes. My heart.

COLORISM

I kept wondering
Why my eyes were once prone to roll
At skin that could pass
The brown paper bag test
I started connecting dots
Every time I won 2nd place
It was to women
Who looked like Billie Holiday

CHURCH BOYS

Ask me if I know any good jokes
And all I'll say is church boys

My body will slowly roll out
of the chair of hurt as laughter
forces its way out of me

I know church boys who have preached
a good word then tried to figure out
which one of the girls they want to lead
astray in the same evening

I know church boys who claim their
favorite scripture is 1 Peter 4:8
While their sweat reeks of Proverbs 26:23

I know church boys who have used the
Lord's name in vain
Said it was because of God they needed
to take their hearts back, ones they never
really gave
When really they were using the cross
to get away with murder
Ironic

The one who abused me in my sleep
was a church boy

The one who used me and confused me
was a church boy

The one who loved me with his lips but hated me
with his heart was a church boy

Ask me if I know any good jokes
And all I'll say is...

GOD

Being alone
With no bodies present in the room
To hide behind
But mine
Leaves me alone
With Him
God
I think the real fear
Is having Him show me
Things about myself
I'm afraid to see

ROAD RAGE

The same hands that raised up to my Savior
Was the same hands used to flip off that man in the car
The one act like he didn't see me trying to merge
I cursed him out so fast
On Saturday
Turned around and spoke in tongues on Sunday
Turned to my neighbor and said "ain't God good"
Monday come
Turned to the car beside me that almost hit me
Saying words that didn't practice what I preach
Same car I used to speed to church when I'm late
Be the same car I used to chase
That Nissan on the freeway
The one that cut me off
Highway patrol pulled me over
God had to pull me over
Told me bury my face in Proverbs
Reckless driving, reckless mouth
At first it didn't seem that deep
But then I learned
My road rage
Spoke of my character

DISTANCE

I cracked the door open
When He knocked
Didn't let Him fully in
Covered my ears and
La la la-ed while He talked to me
Pulled a Jonah
Rather lay my head in a whale
Than to listen
Played a constant game of hide and seek
I kept hiding from Him
Then ran to the corner to sulk
Cuz He ain't answer my prayer

REGRET

Regret
They skip stones together over murky waters
They take long walks down rocky trails and reminisce
about what could have been
What should have been
What would have been had she listened
They argue
Regret reminds her that she put all her eggs in one
basket and it broke
She chokes on its words
I told you so
The truth will set her free, but her bondage is more
comfortable
She's lost herself
An empty body with no soul and a scarred heart
A marred heart, simply existing
Ask her what the meaning of life is
I bet she'll answer you with silence

DIVORCE

I would always feel bad for my friends
Most of them never heard daddy say "go ask your mama"
Cuz mama and daddy were never in the same universe

I had mama & papa come
To open house
To back to school night
To graduation
To everything
Together
Then I turned 25
And became like my friends

QUIT

You called it quits at 24 years
Just shy of 25
That pissed me off
It was like watching a track star
Run hard
Jump over hurdles
Be seconds from the finish line
Then stop to walk away

SPLIT

Last year
I asked myself a question I never asked before
Whose house should I go to for Thanksgiving

SIBLING RIVALRY

I'm not sure why we didn't get along, growing up
I guess it was my fault
All I know is when my little brother
Yelled I hate you
A piece of my soul left that I never thought would
return

BIOLOGICAL

I got a daddy, thank God
But when I found out about the other one
The one science says makes me his
Like a letter with your name on it
Sent to the wrong house
Showed up 16 years later
Change your whole life
I wondered
How come he ain't want me

DADDY ISSUES

Give me a rope
I am the queen of Tug of War
Holding on to something that gives so much resistance

Holding on to something that doesn't want to stay
Men
It's his fault

GRADUATION

17, valedictorian
I graduated college early
Granny says "you got some fans"
Couple kids from nowhere
Show up wanna take pictures
Mama thinks we share the same blood
Look up, he drives by
Throws up the peace sign
Mama whispers to me
Yea
That was your father

LITTLE SISTER

I thought about reaching out to my sister
The one my scientific dad made
With a woman
That wasn't my mother
Around the exact same time he made me

I thought about reaching out to my sister
Remembering how growing up
I always wanted one
But mom and dad kept making boys
I got brothers to wrestle with
But no one to play Barbies

I thought about reaching out to my sister
But then I remembered
Last time her father asked her
Did she want to talk to me
She said "no"

THE COLLEGE DROPOUT

Growing up, they all knew me as the bookworm
They would ask "the Asians"
And me
To copy homework
I felt honored
They heard I went to college at 15
Their jealousy excited me
Fast forward to the present
They got B.A.s
And Masters
And Doctorates
And I'm in debt to a school
Whose stage I ain't even walk
Like paying child support
For a baby that ain't even yours

ENVY

You ever be so envious of someone else's success

Clapping your hands as they dance
across the stage takes too much energy

Letting a congratulations escape your lips
for their promotion is like throwing up razor blades

Smiling as they walk down the aisle
is like taking a knife and forcefully carving happy
onto your face

IDENTITY CRISIS

I've been scared to be a woman
Cuz some of the ones I know
Still healing from years of
Don't talk about it
Hush, they didn't touch you

I've been scared to be black
Cuz I've seen faces that resemble mine
Broken into nothing on asphalt
Become afterthoughts in howling winds
That muffle their cries

I've been scared to be both
I've choked
On fear
Cuz thats all the world feeds me
Anti woman
Anti black
Serve it up on a pretty platter
Bon appétit

RED, WHITE, & BLUE

I have a fear of colors
Red, white, blue
Combined, they send my mind into a million directions
Make me wonder if I served my purpose in life
Make me contemplate the ways in which I will meet
God

A bullet
A beating
One of the above paired with sexual assault
All of it covered up

Make me think about my mother
My father
My brothers
And how they will afford my funeral
How they will survive a world
Trying its hardest to find images
That question my character, integrity

I have a fear of colors
Red, white, blue
Combined, they pulled me over
Sent me to timeout on a cold sidewalk
Made themselves at home in my purse
Felt threatened by my 5'2 frame and called backup
5 more squad cars and dogs bigger than my existence
Became magicians, the way they slowed down time

The way they made a reason to pull me over appear

The way they made me a volunteer for their next act

All because
They have a fear
Of color

CHAMELEON

I think it was after Trayvon
Or Oscar
Or Philando
Or Sandra
Or Eric
Or Korryn
Or Mike
Or Nia
Or the other countless black bodies labeled
target practice

I can't remember
I can't keep track
Of the order in which America became less and less
beautiful
As if it ever really was to begin with

All I can remember is at some point
Walking past white male faces
On the street
At the grocery story
At my job
At church
Made my skin want to hide from my bones
Run for cover
Made my body want to turn chameleon
Change color for protection

PARABLES

Poems be to me
What parables be to Jesus
They came to Him and asked
"Why do you speak to the people in parables?"
He answered them
"Because it has been given to you to know the
mysteries of the kingdom of heaven, but to them it has
not been given"

If you ask me why I write poetry
Why my words come together in ways
The untrained ear or eye cannot understand
Why my tongue speaks sign language instead of
common
It is because my words are not meant for everyone
Some see but do not see
Some hear but do not hear
But one day
The breath that leaves my body will be made clear to all

PSALM
THIRTY
FIVE

STUPID

It all made me who I am now
The fire I played with
Laid with
Stayed with
Couple lessons learned
But sometimes I be lookin' back at her
The old me, like
Yeah
You were stupid

STORMS

I noticed
While it was raining
Pouring
While dark clouds gathered
And tore my world upside down
I had fewer people in my boat
Fighting the waves with me
Than when the sun was shining
On still waters
The day before
Storms be funny like that
Open up your eyes to see
Who don't really love you

FLOWERS

I used to wish I could create my own path
A clean slate with no mess
Just constant rainbows and sunshine
But man made materials are ugly things
Like cement and asphalt
Flowers only bloom with dirt and rain

FORGIVENESS

Yes
I did
The one who ate from the tree
That was to be untouched
Without permission
The one who made me forget my body
belonged to me
The human brain could never comprehend
why
But I did
Turned my bitterness
Into olive branch
I forgave him

THANK YOU

I guess I can thank them
Each one that once brought me to ruin

Good job

Your selfishness helped me learn something

How to be selfish with myself

GRATEFUL

I remember the first time we hung out
I felt like it was going pretty well
Until your other daughter called
Full of attitude
You hung up on her
Called her an animal that walks on all fours
Barks
And instantly
I internally poured out my praise
Thanked God Almighty you didn't raise me

DONOR

Before 8th grade
You were Santa Claus
But less real
No memory of your face was left
In my brain
Lucky me
11 years old
Mama finally played telephone
Whispered in my ear your secret

That you didn't understand math
That you didn't understand aftermath
That you didn't understand the birds
and the bees
That you didn't understand that 1 body
plus 1 body can make 3
That you didn't understand the result of your actions
was me
Yet here I am

27, alive and
Well you had quite the nerve
The spirit of the Fresh Prince's daddy
lives on in you
The hell with you
A child trapped in a man's body
Everything opposite of Cliff Huxtable but
synonymous with Cosby, guilty as charged

I can remember the alarms going off in my head
What did I do
What was wrong with me
Why was a relationship with you as dead as Mariah's

voice carrying through the wind, weightless

Spaceships would be my only mode of transportation to get to you
An unknown species to my world
An alien alienating his duty, fleeing pride rock to not take his rightful place as dad
But rather taking the place of scars
decorating my heart

Perpetuating the stereotypical cycle that black men don't take care of their kids
Black men don't take care of their offspring
Black men leave little girls and little boys with the haunting message that if daddy didn't want you, good luck with the rest of the world

That was my misperception because of you
2 weeks ago the doctor asked me about my family medical history
And I couldn't truthfully answer, because there were branches to my tree I never got the chance to sit on

You are to me what impossible is to God
Nothing
But a loaner
You loaned her
Pieces of you
The seed that fell among thorns but bloomed into everything not statistic
I survived

Realized I was deprived of you so that God could give me an upgrade
Shout out to the government for my last name transplant
Shout out to Papa Kelly

The embodiment of everything a father should be
Everything you are not
Everything you have taught me comes down to one
thing

That running is never an option
It is but a concoction of fear,
2 cups of immaturity, a tablespoon of laziness, and a
splash of pathetic
Running is never an option
It is but an entree of mixed emotions, 100 grams of
coward, and 4 ounces of weak
Thank God I never ate from the plate you served
me, or else I'd still be hungry

And see at first glance
This poem sounds angry
This poem sounds likes the writer's heart has gone sour
A bitter taste left in a mouth full of whys
But I promise you it is the complete opposite
Would you believe a year ago I wouldn't have even been
able to voice what my insides have been screaming for
so long
So long to that spirit of fear
So long to that spirit of abandonment
So long to that tight grip I've had all my life on men
who really wanted to leave
You can leave

So long to the hours spent staring in dirty mirrors
wondering was it me
It wasn't me
It wasn't me
It wasn't me

TECHNICALLY

I hate explaining the story
The one where people learn my father came into my
life when I was already born, though I didn't know it
They always say "so technically, that's your step dad"
I tell them
"No, that's my dad"

RELATIONSHIP

How can you know someone
If you only acquaint yourself
With opinions of them

I grew up in church
They been telling me for years
Who Jesus was
I had to get to know Him myself

ROOTS

I want my ears
to be so familiar with
His voice
His touch
His presence

that when you hear me speak
all you see
is His heart

that when my feet decide to move
they only do so
at His command

-Colossians 2:7

FAMILY

Eat dinner at the table
Watch Jeopardy
Play Life
Pack snacks for a day at the park
Light candles in the dark
Whatever we did
We did it
Together

BROTHERS

Tommy
Jonathan
They came after me
Over 5 years apart
I remember thinking
How could I ever connect
With people that seem light years away
Now
I can't imagine life without them

MAMA

Day in
Day out
She sings them into the ground
Seeds, three of them
Later spring into royalty
Waters them with her sweat
And love
Tired yet relentless, she works
Shoulders heavy
Feet aching
She will break her everything
Just to see each flower she plants bloom

PAPA

I remember I once wrote in my journal
I hate you
Wished you to be like other parents
More free, yet blind
But no
Your feet were statues
Grounded
You modeled parenthood
After God
Took the anger
Attitude
Blame
Even if it meant protecting me
From the monsters under my bed
I couldn't see
I feel sorry for the people
Who don't get to call you dad

OCTOBER 8TH

I hope you don't mind that I shared a piece of you with
the world
I just remember how I felt when you said
You're divorcing
Felt like someone took all the family photos
Cut them up
But prayer changes things
You glued the photos back together
Got remarried
My tears smiled and laughed
October 8th is one of my favorite days

FAILURE VS REGRET

Her eager feet trotted to the space where sand meets water
She walked out and sank
Lips stretching from west to east as she swam back to surface
She had never been happier
To almost drown
At least she tried

I AM HERE

Drop me in the deepest darkest part of the ocean
Where even evil hides in fear
And pray the waters wash away my existence
You could never drown my spirit

Wrap my neck in the strongest rope your hands could
find
Pulling & suffocating until tears race down my face
And wait for my fiery soul to separate from my body
You could never control my voice

Strip me of everything every human being deserves
Love, respect, understanding
Leave me standing naked with nothing but laughter
seeping into my ears
You could never take away my dignity
I am here, we are here
Here to stay

REFLECTION

You know you've accepted yourself
When you can finally look into a mirror
For longer than 5 minutes
Without breaking it
I am whole

CLICHE

I've heard
One of the best things
For a woman to do
After she picks herself
And her heart up off the floor
Is to Delilah herself
Take her glory
And trade it in for peace
Cutting off my hair
And them
Was more than just the best decision
It was the only one

BREATHE

Let the ground kiss your back

Open sky

Closed eyes

Inhale, exhale

Let it go

SMILE

Let your tears flow until your soul becomes a desert
Then realize you still have breath & smile
Your heart deserves to laugh

CREDIT

After 8 rounds of bloody noses
Ears that needed draining
Eyes that felt as swollen as your heart
Feet that were close to broken
As they all watched
You stayed in the ring
Give yourself a little credit

TESTIMONY

I didn't tell you
that most of my decisions
to turn away
from God
happened after I met Him,

or that I used to dive into pools
of anger and rage,

or that my mind and feet
have traveled to places
my soul
begged them not to,

or that the heart I gifted
to many was returned to me
damaged,

just for you to pat me
on the back
and congratulate me for making it,
or pull out your banner of
"it was all you."

Don't let your disbelief
of Him
keep you from hearing truth.

I told you these things to show you
after all of it,
or rather in the midst of it,
the one my soul now longs for

never took His hand off me.

Ask me how I made it.
And watch my heart fall
to its knees,
lift its arms in awe
of the only one
capable enough
to love me out.

HABITS

It be funny
How I made it out alive
Few scars that eventually faded
With prayer, time, and cocoa butter
I made people proud I didn't even know were watching

But those cycles
Just because they've been broken
Don't mean they can't be put back
together
New struggles
New mistakes
I still got bad habits to break

CONFIDENCE

I got so used to hearing my thoughts
Yell ugly things like

YOU CAN'T
YOU WON'T
YOU'RE LESS THAN

That my ears had to be trained to hear
YOU CAN

FRIENDS

I had to learn to channel
Anger
Rejection
Fear
Into something that didn't involve
Mean mugging potential friends
I need you

HOPE

I was professor and student
Taught myself the art of expecting less
Better to know the rain is coming
And be surprised with sunshine
Than vice versa
I rehearsed a thousand times
My lines
Let my brain memorize the formula
Life
Minus dreams and hope
Equals safe
What a way
To not live

IDOLS

I used to beg for love
From men
More times than He said forgiven
To me
Things are different now
Men are no longer the object of my repentance
I already have a God

I AIN'T SORRY

When I was 17 years old
My boyfriend broke up with me
He had finally made a decision to be with
his brother's sister that wasn't really his sister
That's a whole 'nother issue

His reason was that he "knew her longer than me"
I reached into my emotional cabinet on tippy toes
and grabbed my bag of sorries
Took one out and wrapped it in the prettiest bow
He accepted it
As if it was money he had loaned me
and was waiting for

Not long after, he asked me to be his girlfriend
again
I said yes
It wasn't long before he pushed me
like I was on the swing at the park
Into the table at his mama's house
I stood up
Snatched my earrings off my ears so fast
Put on my invisible vaseline and socked him
in his mouth
At least that's what I wish I did
Instead, I reached into my back pocket
Pulled out a travel size sorry and placed it
in his hand
Watched him crumble it into pieces

When I was 23 years old
I was months away from being proposed to
Little did I know I was also months away

from calling off my wedding
To a man, or rather a boy,
who shouldn't have been my man in the first place
I gave him all the sorries he actually owed me
Let him lay up on the couch that I paid for
In the apartment that I paid for
Eating food
That I paid for
Let him yell at me for hounding him
about the $120 he said he'd pay me back
a week ago

I reached into my makeup bag
Took some red lipstick and drew on a smile
Whispered I'm sorry
When really I wanted to say
Negro this is my house
Pack what little you have and go sleep
in your car
You wouldn't be nothing if it wasn't for me
But my soul convinced me I was too weak
So I did what I do best
Fixed him a plate of sorry and served it up
on the prettiest platter I could find

When I was 24 years old
On my first day at my new job
A man bumped into me in the hallway
I quickly swallowed my pride
Told it to stay in its room and don't come out
until I said so
As I easily threw up a sorry to give him
You could have sworn I was homeless
The way he worked so hard to not make eye contact
with me and kept walking

3 weeks later

It was groundhog day
Almost felt like I should have been singing
Beyonce
The way Deja Vu appeared
The same man bumped me
And without thinking, I channeled
my inner woman
At least the version of woman this world
tells me to be
I said sorry to his unapologetic soul with ease

When I was 26 years old
A friend
Became a close friend
Became more than a friend
Disguised as a "best friend"
Sold me packaged dreams that broke as soon
as I got home and opened the box
Shape shifted into Aladdin
Told me he could show me the world
When all he showed me was how ugly he really was
Whispered I love you so no one else could hear
Treated me like guilty pleasure
An object he didn't want folk to know he wanted
He would vomit lie after lie after lie
And I'd become dog
Eat it up as if it was the only food I deserved

I finally confronted him about his secrets
How I didn't deserve to be told I could be his wife
While his words spoke the same to another
innocent woman
How he could not call me "best friend"
and treat me the worst
He stoned me with sorries then laughed afterward
with his actions
Turned around and did it all again

And again
And again

I never really apologized to him
At least not with my words
But with my body
My hands
My eyes
My heart
I cried a million sorries for not being
good enough

When I was 27 years old
I finally understood that sorry was too readily
available to spill from my lips
From my stomach
I treated sorry the way people have treated me
Overly used and losing its worth

The moral of the story is to understand
That sorry is not always owed
Sorry is not to be given to folk
who dismiss your emotions
It is not a trade off for those
who can't acknowledge their own wrong
No longer will I repent to men on behalf
of their own immaturity

Sorry had me doing too much
Like I was both plaintiff and defendant
Put myself on trial for somebody else's mistakes
Sorry got me messed up
Helped me realize that it is time for women
to stop apologizing for existing
For feeling sad
For feeling happy
For feeling angry

For feeling weak
For feeling strong
Our sorries are reserved for people
who actually deserve them

So I guarantee you
The next time you hear me say it
It will be because I actually did wrong
Not because an apology is currency
Serving as the means to buy a man's
attention
Or time
Or love
Or respect
Beyonce said it best
I ain't sorry

AGAPE

Imagine my surprise when I told Him
that the blood He shed for me
did not concern me, with my actions.
And He looked me in my eyes and said
"Yet, I still love you."

THE CHASE

Only
man
worth
chasing
took nails into hands, into feet and went
before
thousands
humbly
screamed
I
love
you
with
His
body

WAITING

After all of it
Swimming in my own river
Of tears
For hours on end
I finally got out
Wrinkles and all

Learned things like
Worth
And value
And patience

Yet and still
I'm waiting
For him
The one we all dream of

FAITH

Common sense says you can't trust a God
who allowed you to go through heartache.
Heartbreak.
Pain.

Faith says do it anyway.
He was there in the fire the whole time.

MY TYPE

My type of man
Is the one who will stay up
Til 2 in the morning on Halloween
Making his daughter angel wings from scratch
Because all the stores ran out

The one who will make
His daughter a board game
To help her learn multiplication

The one who will cancel his morning run
To comfort his daughter and her nightmares
After reading books she had no business reading

My type of man will treat his daughter
The way my father did me

HIDDEN

Tired
of seeing
them find their
yes when all I've
found is my everlasting
no. So I yelled from the bottom
of my hurt to God, "Where is my
husband!" He took my hand and told
me, "Hidden. I don't want you to spill
your broken on him. Let's make you whole first."

LIFE GOES ON

I've hurt people
Turned my mouth into a flowing river

Of apology
Transformed my eyes into arms

And silently screamed forgive me
To people who forgot they once screamed

Forgive me to others
To God

Their bodies became Neo
Dodged every sorry I sang to them

But I sleep very well at night
Don't cry over spilled hypocrisy

ME

When you love hard, others
It be easy
To forget to save some
For yourself

I come from serving them 3 course meals
Then sitting at the table hungry
From showering them with encouragement
Then being left with no hot water
From pulling out chairs for them to sit
Then finding a seat on the floor
From spending all my time on them
Then filing for bankruptcy

Eventually
I had to get selfish
I had to choose
Me

CONFESSION

I've learned the art of telling on myself
I don't do it for applause
I do it for them
The ones who think they're alone
Struggling in secret can become exhausting
I'll come out of hiding if it means someone else can
too

WALK AWAY

She said to me
"I'm dating your ex"
In the race to who could say
"And I care why" the fastest
My mouth could not keep up with my face

My stomach started laughing and my eyes said
hold it, at least until you walk away
I found words to say and used some of them
Described my experience in a movie trailer
Long enough to express truth but short enough
to get to the point

She wanted to relive middle school
Eat lunch then head to the bleachers to indulge
in gossip for dessert
I ate some of the icing but threw the cake away

Revenge said paint her a picture of as much
of the ugly as you can in 3 minutes
But character said leave the canvas blank
Wish her the best
Walk away

PROVERBS 28:13

Keep making the same one, and a mistake
soon becomes second nature
I don't speak from false wisdom
I speak from unnecessary experience
My flesh opposed spirit so heavy
Sin started to look like sound doctrine
Funny the way I used to mock them
"I would never" tattooed across my chest
My back never sat straighter

Then finally I let pride trip me
Turn me into hypocrite
Opened the door to my downfall
I learned that from Solomon
Only I didn't really learn it
The bridge between me & God
Condemnation made me think I burned it
Fallen angel whispers lies like
"Kill yourself, cuz His grace, you'll never earn it"

Keep telling the same one, and a lie
soon becomes your reflection
Only Jesus succeeded at what's humanly
unattainable, perfection
I used to lay the hands that held my heart
on a hot stove, smiling, whispering
"It's not that bad" to my 3rd degree burned soul
She is clothed in strength & dignity
tattooed down my back but when no one
was watching
I took clothes off for the wrong reason
The irony

Iron the wrinkles in my image & make it look crisp
for the camera
Filter the blemishes
Crop out the ugly so all the world sees
is an edited version of me
But eventually
All that lying
All that mask
All that secret
Gon' come out
What's done in the dark
Comes to the center stage, spotlight on
Lights, camera, exposure

No one's exempt
We all got the potential to be imposter
Dressing up dirt, make it look pretty, prim,
and proper
Can't be healed if you don't reveal your symptoms
to doctor
He who conceals His sin and don't confess
don't prosper

FREE WILL

No one ever held a gun up to my head and said
Stay
Cry
Hurt
Lie
Smile
Die

I knew that road would burn my feet
And I walked it anyway
Now I've truly learned that free will comes with prices
Consequences
Sacrifice
Responsibility

LESSONS LEARNED

When I came to pick her up
For the 100th time
From jail
She walked out on crutches
Bandages adorning her face
Tears in her eyes
I asked her, my heart, if she had learned
her lesson

She slowly replied, lips parched from
her thirst for love,
"Yes. You're in charge now."

SUNSHINE

If you told me I'd be where I am today
5 years ago
My broken heart would have laughed so hard
Followed by a river of tears streaming down my
mask
I wasn't feeling me, wasn't feeling free
A child of God living like a pauper instead of
a daughter of the king

I once took my body and devalued it
Likened it to that of a road after the first rain
Most accidents happen on the road after the first rain
I know pain
I know pain, I know pain, I know hurt
I know what it feels like to smile so that they don't
see you drowning in a pool of depression
I know what it is to be depressed yet be so
black woman, I can't show it
To be so broken but don't know it
To have a garden but don't grow it

I've stood in rooms full of sunshine but saw only
darkness
I've given away a heart that
Each time returned to me more hardened
I have loved people who hurt me more than 1000
paper cuts
Burned me worse than hand over open flame
I've been Beyonce, Kelly, Michelle, Farrah
Asked him to say my name, say my name
Asked him to change
Let him clothe me in shame
Shape shifted into scapegoat

Body sore from carrying all the blame

I have been Oprah with my apologies when I had
nothing to be sorry for
I have conceived sorrow
Given birth to emptiness
And aborted my purpose
But yet and still
I am a testimony
I am what it looks like when broken and faith
enter matrimony

This be my testament
Back in the old testament
He told me He knew me before He even formed me
Took me out of my lamentations, back to Jeremiah
had a purpose for me

Then in John He warned me
I'd never be immune to falling
Never be immune to stumbling over my calling
Never be immune to trouble and doubt
It's what I do in the midst of it that really counts
I have been asked how I got this far
How I live when my spirit almost died
When my words always cried
When I'd given up the fight

He found me
They think I'm crazy for speaking and praying
to a God I can't see
But faith be
The evidence of things unseen
If only they saw the things I've seen
Every fiber of their being would stand tall
Hands lifted to the God of all
I'm here simply because He brought

the sunshine.

ETERNITY

Yesterday,
my soul told my mind to tell my heart

stop making decisions that make her take
40 steps back.

We have eternity to think of.

REMEMBER

Even when every carnal piece of my being refuses to walk with Him, I speak over myself

Remember why you exist

PHOENIX

They say the phoenix
Is a mythological creature
They must not know bout me

All the heartache, suffering
The pain I've owned in a box
To the left

Finally left it outside to be picked up
With the rest of the trash
I've allowed my soul to hoard
No more

I traded in broken feet for wings
Let the hurt burn me to ash
I've never felt more alive
Than when I was on fire

A SEAT AT THE TABLE

I don't want to spend eternity wondering
who I could have helped had my lips
not listened when fear said be quiet.

My story is not something I just whipped up in the
kitchen to feed myself.

It is a feast I want to invite as many people possible to.

To sit at a table with other imperfect people and break
truth together.

Increasing appetites for a God that will satisfy their
hunger.

I am praying for your victory.

YOU ARE NOT THEM

God didn't use a point of reference to create you.

You are not them and that's okay.
You are not them and that's okay.
You are not them and that's okay.

FOR YOU

This is for the ones who stare at mirrors
And sometimes see ugly

This is for the ones who cross the street
And sometimes think about walking on red

This is for the ones who go to bathroom stalls
And sometimes use them as a place to drain tears

This is for the ones who lay in bed at 2am
And sometimes question the meaning of life

This is for the ones who are at the edge of the cliff

Who feel they have nothing
Who hear nothing but jump
Who see the ground smiling up at them
Who smell the end and lean toward its fragrance
Who taste peace one flatline away
Ready for eternal silence

I used to be you
Not long ago
A dreamer who stopped dreaming
But something came and fought
The sadness off of me
Hope
There's some for you too

OPEN LETTER TO GRANNY

They spun pirouettes in your brain for minutes at a time, the lost cells, taking you away from the present. Sometimes you lived in a different realm than the rest of us. The family dog had died years ago yet sometimes you'd see her.

I remember hearing how you flipped the house upside down in search of reading glasses. Somebody moved your glasses but they actually sat on your head.

Remember your conversations with the girl under the table that only made herself visible to you. People wondered who it was you'd talk to.

I would have loved to walk through the fields of your mind. To pick flowers. Flowers that didn't really exist.

Living in and out of dimensions only accessible to a beautiful mind.

4 years past your ascension into peace and I find guilt, sadness, hurt, still growing on the window panes of my heart like uncontrollable mold.

Shoulda, coulda, woulda becomes my anthem, my sad song.

I shoulda came to see you more.
I coulda spent more time.
If I woulda stopped focusing on me myself and I
If I could press rewind...

And go back to that scene when you were still alive.
When I knew I'd show you my first book.
When I knew we'd take pictures together at my wedding.
When I knew your future great grandchildren would beg to come over.
When I knew you were invincible. That nothing could stop you.
Not even that enemy that once tried to take your womanhood, cancer.

But life took you in its unreliable arms and dropped you. It sat back and laughed as I gasped for a hand to reach down and pick my jaw up off the floor. That disorderly disease dementia, preying on a brain I selfishly knew was everlasting. Yesterday I found myself angrily laughing at the sun because its light couldn't reach the shadows of your mind.

And though there is much about this life I can enjoy, sometimes I can't wait to die. It would mean my heart would once again become full. It would mean my soul would stay happy.

It would mean my eyes could be as opened as Eve's when she ate from that tree. It would mean I would finally get to walk through the fields in your mind and dance pirouettes with you.
Seeing everything we thought didn't exist.

PURIFICATION

I was pushed into the fire
Skin deep fried
Burned like hell
Like if the sun left his throne in the sky
To dance with me
It hurt
Funny, it took pain to take the pain away
I swam in an ocean of flames
Returned to the rose garden as gold
Beautiful things don't always start out beautiful
Sometimes the best things come from ugly

PILLOW TALK

I got into bed, ready to close my eyes and dream
My body whispered thank you
I asked what it had to be thankful for
It said "for slowly, but surely, letting me become
whole."

I AM

A woman
A black woman
A black woman who loves
A black woman who loves Jesus
A black woman who loves Jesus and life
Writes poetry and stories
Plays violin
and piano
Dances
Sings
Draws
Enjoys tv
and movies
and video games
and board games
and people
Likes laughing
Likes to get others laughing
Is wild
Is loud
Is nervous
Is outgoing
Is real
Is proud
Is scared
Is bold
Is organized
Is messy
Is funny
Is serious
Is lighthearted
Is deep

Is encouraging
Is caring
Is hopeful
Is doubtful
Is brown
Is tattooed
Is bald
Is beautiful
Is weird
Is crazy
Is me
Is me
Is me
Is soup
Is bowl
Of surprise
Everything
In between
Apologizes for what
Apologizes for nothing
I am
A woman
A black woman
A black woman who loves
A black woman who loves Jesus
A black woman who loves Jesus and life

2 KINDS OF FIRE

There are 2 kinds of fire
Both painful in process

Makes the soul feel like it's paying
for someone else's mistakes
Makes the feet wonder where they went wrong

The first
Heavy handed
A king of purging
Removing every unfruitful tree by the root
Burning away all things toxic
Thoughts
Habits
Mindsets
People
Feels like God is a black mother
Plays the "I'm doing this because I love you" card

The second, a teacher
Pushes you to limits your mind says no to
But your spirit desperately needs
A 100 degree celsius Jordan River
Baptizing
Strengthening
Purifying
The body, inside out
Sometimes feels like you're in it alone
Until you realize someone else was in it with you
The whole time

There are two kinds of fire

Both painful in process
That is, until you walk out
Strong
Whole
Protected
Bold
Free

And here we are.
At the end.
If the words on these pages triggered you at all,
I am relieved.

It means you are human.
It means you have walked or are still walking through
some healing of your own.
And that is okay.
Get ready for the beauty that you are soon to be.
You're already on your way.

I pray that you find the strength, courage, and even joy
to share your own story. To find freedom in refusing to
be silent about who you've been, who you are, and who
you are becoming.

If you were touched by this book, I would love to hear
from you.

Write to me at info@thepoeticactivist.com
or send me a message on
Instagram & Facebook.

Take a photo of your favorite poem and tag me on
Instagram (@thepoeticactivist).

Share this book with someone else who needs to know
they aren't alone. Someone who needs some hope.

Thank you for listening to my story.
I hope to one day hear yours.

ABOUT THE AUTHOR

Porsche N. Kelly is an artist, activist, speaker, and influencer from Oakland, Ca. Her poetry is full of raw conviction, as she unapologetically spreads messages filled with truth and transparency.

Porsche's writing focuses on social justice, faith, and personal life, intentionally allowing the three to intersect. While most of her work consists of poetry, her love for short stories and fiction remains, which will be evident in her debut fiction novel.

For more information on Porsche's work, events, and upcoming projects, visit www.thepoeticactivist.com and follow on Instagram: @thepoeticactivist.